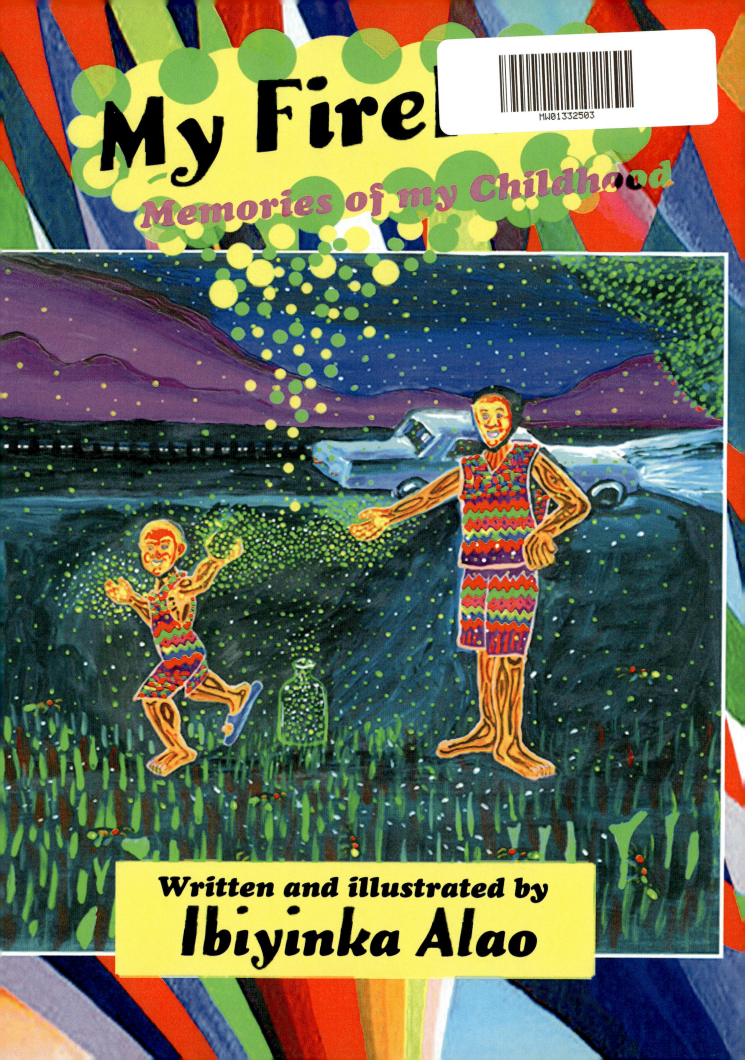

Reviews are wonderful!

Today I met a wonderous human being, who speaks with the beautiful language of art through his vibrant paintings. I'm thrilled that the children in our school have had the chance to meet Ibi and feel the life spark from his persona as well as his brightly-coloured art work. I can't wait to see the art work that the children produce in his homage. It was a joy to meet a United Nations art prize winner and art ambassador who so perfectly embodies the meaning of being creative.

- Claire Hodgson
Headteacher
Burstow Primary School,
London

There are painters that are said to be naive - often they are great poets who are magical and majestic witnesses. They see the things that pass unnoticed by ordinary eyes. They have the ability to narrate wordless stories about nature and the harmony of things gracefully. Their paintings are songs for the evening. The truth that you see in them will first make you smile, but then it will disturb the most sceptical of observers. Their paintings are too serious, or too scary, no doubt, that is why they are compared to innocent children. Ibiyinka carries his tranquillity the same way as those who know the mysteries of the World.

- Pascal Letellier

Pascal Letellier is a poet and was Director of the French Cultural Center, Lagos, Nigeria where he met Ibiyinka and hosted an exhibition of his paintings in celebration of Yoruba proverbs

"Thank you, Mr. Alao.... for making me reflect on the universal language of art"

- Andrew Wyeth,
American Painter,
May, 2005.

Andrew Wyeth's paintings *"Christina's World"* and *"Wind from the Sea"* influenced Ibiyinka's work during his formative years as an artist. After winning the UN art prize and traveling to the United States, Wyeth saw some of the young artist's works like *"The Music Party"* and *"Mortal Feelings"* arranged through a curator at the Brandywine River Valley Museum of Art in 2005.

In loving memory of my father,
Ezekiel Bamisaiye Alao.

For Grace Bosede, Makanjuola,
Feyisike, Olusola, Omowumi,
who gave me hope
and Kaila,
who made me Love.

Introduction

In 2006, I painted a picture with many parts I called, Eternity in Our Hearts. It is based on a true story about my childhood love of fireflies and stars. In 2016, I showed this painting to some school children and explained its deeper meaning. Their gifted teacher asked my permission to present it as their entry to that year's Scholastic Kids Are Authors Writing Contest. "Ibi's Fireflies" won the grand prize and is now a book published by Scholastic Book Fairs. I am very thankful to this teacher at Willow Lane Elementary School and Scholastic for taking a chance on my story. I had kept this story in my writer's jar since its creation in 2006 and would often tell it from memory. Now I am setting it free. This is my original story about one unforgettable night filled with fireflies and stars from my childhood.

- Ibi

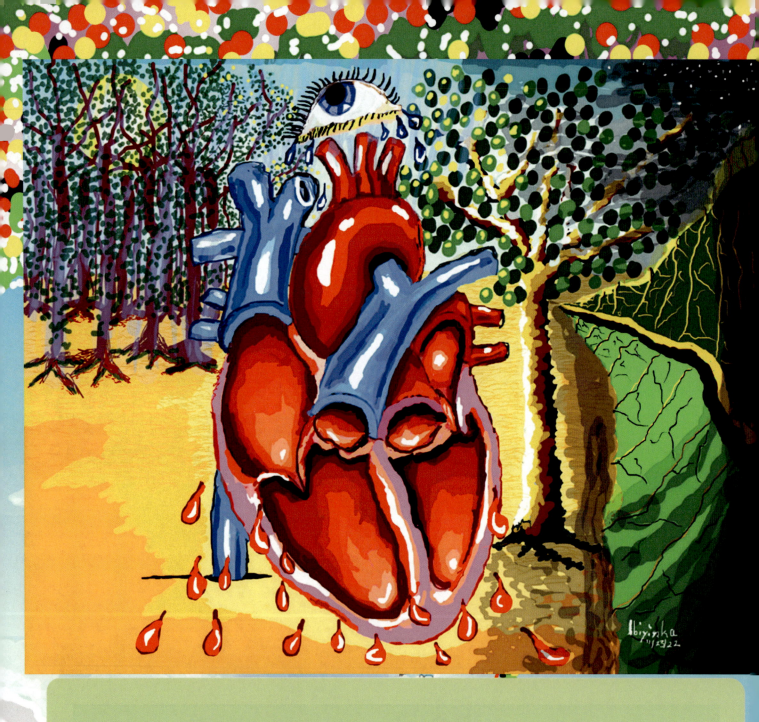

The heart is like a jar containing fireflies, and love happens when we let those fireflies go on to become stars.

To begin, let us imagine that the heart is a jar full of fireflies, and that love is something invisible coming out from that jar which turns fireflies into stars. It might not make sense right now, but it will by the end of this story.

The human heart and fireflies have something in common.
The sun, human beings, animals and leaves all go to sleep.
Darkness takes a hold of the night; the world is silent.
But out come fireflies and the heart keeps beating - here, there.
It sounds - lub dub, lub dub, lub dub - on and on and on.
There is no companion that sees like the heart;
it speaks to God, it speaks to us, it knows the truth.
Everything is clear to the aorta of the heart.

It sings a song that yearns for freedom. Fireflies are creatures who yearn for freedom, too. As indicator species, they sense a healthy environment and go there. They are a light to the world just as the heart is the light of the soul.

I am an artist. In my childhood, I enjoyed catching fireflies and looking up at the stars. They both fascinated me. Whenever I looked up to the sky, I made pictures out of stars by connecting the dots in my mind.

Some pictures are stories that mean different things at different times of our lives. It's not that they are better painted than others. They are just sparked by something extra. In telling this story from my childhood, it's impossible to separate reality from imagination. It neither has a beginning and an end, nor does it have a distinct storyline which makes sense to the world, but that's exactly what kind of story this is.

One day, my father drove me home from his work as he usually did. It was a beautiful night full of stars and an endless dark blue sky.

As we were heading
back home in his car
on this particular night
of a thousand stars,
I saw a cluster of fireflies
on the side of the road.

I said to him, "Daddy, look! Fireflies!" I had said it in a way children would sometimes say to their moms and dads whenever they saw a favorite toy store, or ice-cream shop, or even candy store. You said it out loud, but didn't always expect them to stop everything just because you wish them to.

What a beautiful thing it is though if an adult listens to and stops everything to honor the simple, honest inner desires of a child! In fact, what a beautiful thing it is when one human being can slow down, listen and stop to honor the hopes of another.

To my surprise, not only did my father stop the car, but he reversed it back to the spot where the fireflies were and pulled out a transparent jar from the trunk. He handed this jar to me and said that I could go into the bush, catch all the fireflies I wanted and put them inside.

For a boy who loves fireflies, this was like heaven. I was allowed to catch the fireflies and my father was helping me. We ran all over the bush, catching as many fireflies as we could keep. We were catching treasures and finding light in unusual places. It was a spectacular sight!

My fireflies lived in my jar for a while that night. They flew around and lit up my face as they hit the walls of the jar with their light. I loved those fireflies and held them close, speaking words of friendship to them. Together, we traveled to a beautiful world of dreams. Humans live a long time, but not so for fireflies.

After a while, their lights began to dim. My father told me to let my fireflies go. I bent my head in sadness. I thought to myself that without my sparkling friends I could not see the beauty of that night.

Even though I was sad when my father told me to let my fireflies go, it wasn't for long. He gave me a reason that inspires me as an artist to use dots in painting the many stars in my pictures. My father could have said, "Let the fireflies go, otherwise they will die!" But he never gave such simple answers to such things. Instead he said, "If you don't let the fireflies go, then you will never see stars in the sky again. In the middle of the night, when we all go to sleep, fireflies turn into stars. So, if you want to keep seeing stars in the sky, every time you catch fireflies, you must let them go."

You can say this is not true, but it made sense to me on that starry night. I believed my father, because glancing up at the stars, and looking at my fireflies in the jar, I couldn't tell the difference. They both twinkled and sparkled. Besides, it cheered me up as I was exchanging the fireflies I loved, for the stars I adored. So I opened the jar and let the fireflies go free. They twinkled as they disappeared into the stars. I couldn't tell where the fireflies ended and the stars began. It was a magnificent contrast of light and darkness. The whole world seemed to be held in a dreamlike bliss. It was a magical night, and it was in that moment I knew the transformative power of a vision.

Long after this night, every time I went to bed, I saw fireflies transfigured into stars on the inside of my eyelids. I was still fascinated by fireflies but whenever I caught them, I did not want to keep them in a jar, instead I tried to push them up with my hands so that they could become the stars they were meant to be.

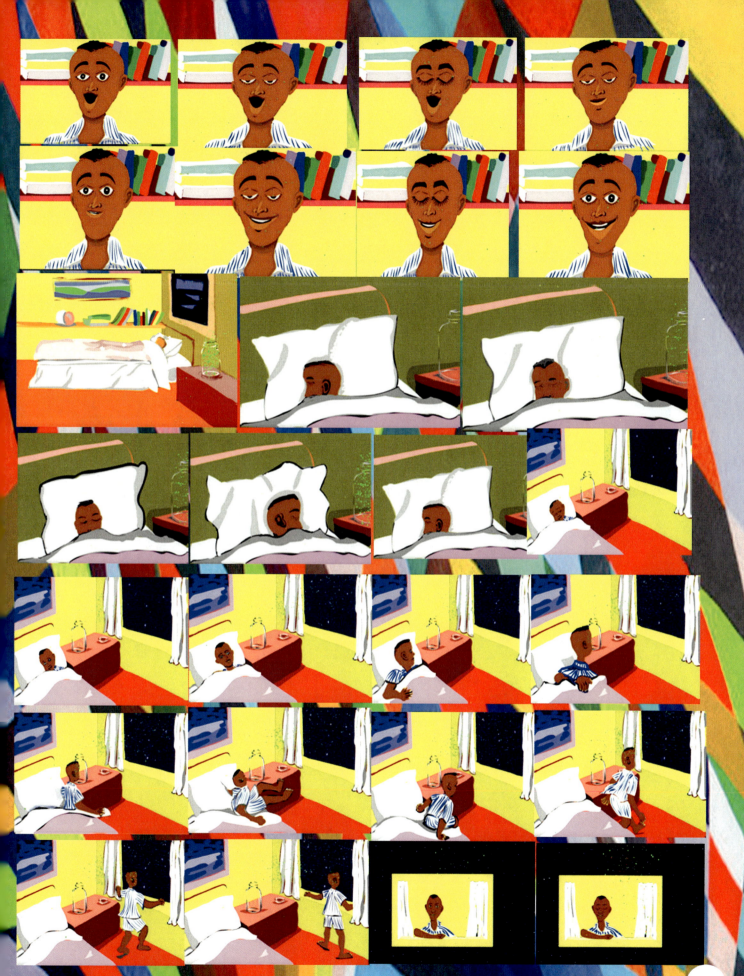

Although I realize now that fireflies don't actually become stars, my father taught me an important lesson that evening. When you love something as much as I loved those fireflies, the best thing to do is to let it go free. Only then would it become a bright star shining down on me forever.

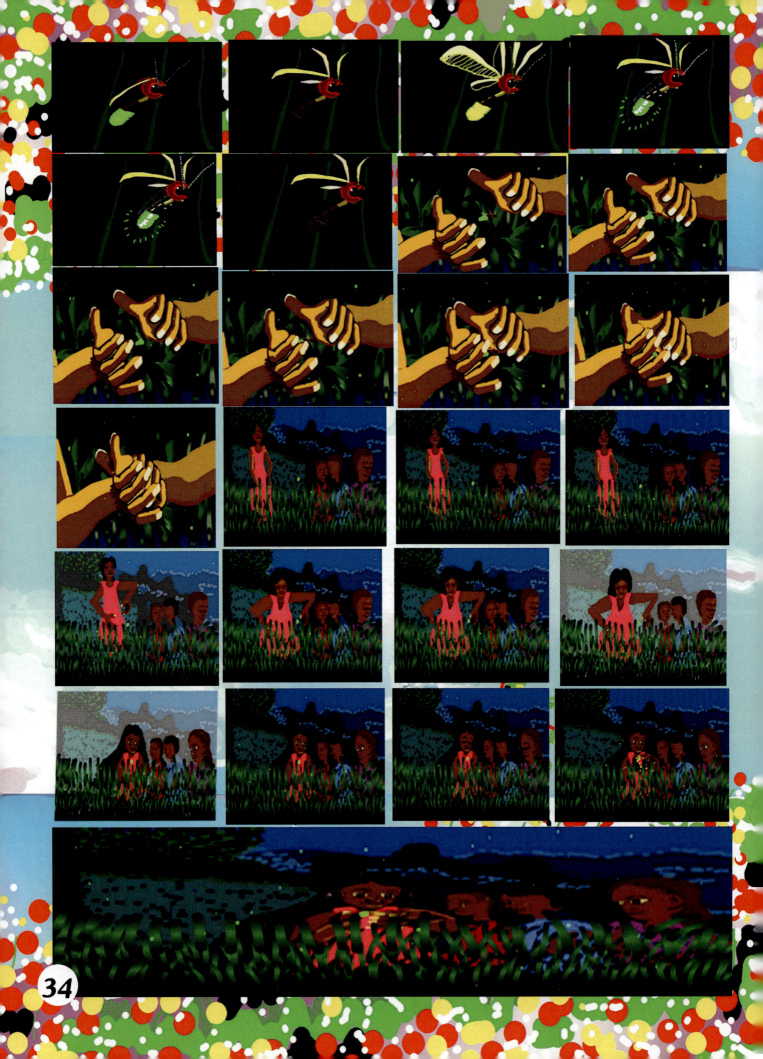

There are many lessons of love to learn from my fireflies story. Lessons are like treasures and my original painting for this story comprises many. Here, you may use your imagination to find these treasures. One is to imagine fireflies actually becoming stars of the universe as shown in this painting.

Girl with Red Hair releasing her Fireflies for Stars in the Milky Way Galaxy

The soft light of a different world shone upon her red hair. When she let her Fireflies go, it seemed to her that they became Stars of their own. Everything was moving but not in the Earthly motion way we are used to. They moved in slow motion, yet they travelled at the Speed of light. Each firefly had an escape velocity capable of catapulting it so high that it became a new light in the firmament of our Universe. This Light grew brighter and brighter as the Jar she held became darker and faded away. At one moment she wept, and the Stars alone remained. The whole thing reminded her of a Supernova - That is new stars are born when an old star is destroyed. If there's any truth to learn, if there's any hope to believe, it is that by letting go of a cherished thing, we gain a new and more vibrant version of that thing. By letting go of war, we gain peace. By letting go of slavery, we gain Freedom. By not being possessive of Earth, we reduce the effects of climate change. By loving another human being and allowing them freedom of choice, we gain the true meaning of Love. By letting go of her fireflies, she gained the more permanent stars of the Milky Way Galaxy. And if each star represented a life she had known, of her ancestors and loved ones, what a beautiful constellation of stars they made.

I'll close this story with "Memories of My Childhood," a painting I made to celebrate the warm golden sunset light of Africa, the freedom to choose, and being content in life. It's a picture within a picture. A setup with children playing near the water under the light. One picture has a half moon monkey bar inserted around the children playing, while the other one doesn't. Are you upset about this? How reminiscent of life itself this is. We may have some gadgets to play with in life or we may have life itself to play with. In either case, life is a beautiful sport if we are content with gaining something, or letting go of it.

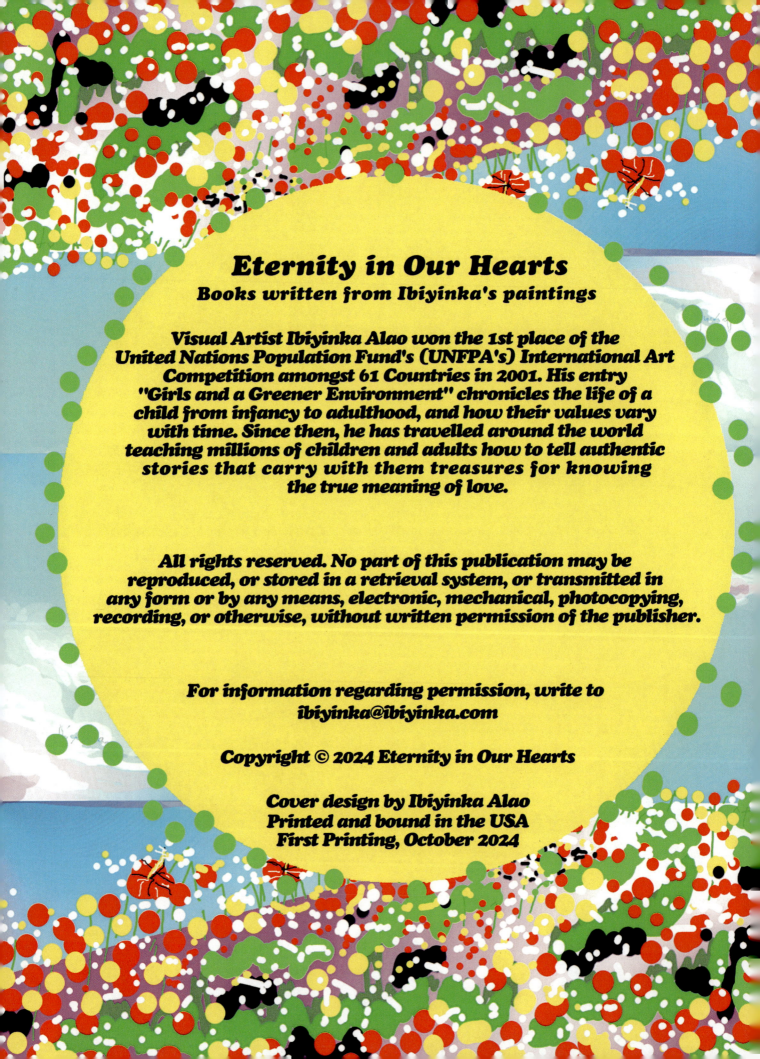

Eternity in Our Hearts
Books written from Ibiyinka's paintings

Visual Artist Ibiyinka Alao won the 1st place of the United Nations Population Fund's (UNFPA's) International Art Competition amongst 61 Countries in 2001. His entry "Girls and a Greener Environment" chronicles the life of a child from infancy to adulthood, and how their values vary with time. Since then, he has travelled around the world teaching millions of children and adults how to tell authentic stories that carry with them treasures for knowing the true meaning of love.

All rights reserved. No part of this publication may be reproduced, or stored in a retrieval system, or transmitted in any form or by any means, electronic, mechanical, photocopying, recording, or otherwise, without written permission of the publisher.

For information regarding permission, write to
ibiyinka@ibiyinka.com

Copyright © 2024 Eternity in Our Hearts

Cover design by Ibiyinka Alao
Printed and bound in the USA
First Printing, October 2024

Made in the USA
Middletown, DE
26 March 2025

73311583R00026